PIANO FOR ADULTS
LEVEL TWO

by WESLEY SCHAUM

Teacher Consultants: Alfred Cahn, Joan Cupp, Sue Pennington

INDEX

SCHAUM PUBLICATIONS, INC.
10235 N. Port Washington Rd.   Mequon, WI 53092

01-52
HD-4

FOREWORD

This method is tailored for an <u>older individual</u> — adult or teen-ager. It may also be used for mature students of a younger age.

The progress here is <u>much more gradual than other adult methods</u>. This allows the student to be entirely comfortable with the learning steps. The rate of progress is flexible; work in this book can be leisurely or fast paced, depending upon the individual pupil and preference of the teacher.

The musical excerpts are themes from symphonies, operas, ballets, concertos, oratorios, chamber music, vocal and choral literature. Also included are folk songs from many ethnic groups. No simplified *piano* music is used. Music appreciation stories of the music and biographical information and portraits of the composers are provided.

Emphasis is placed on <u>analysis of simple musical form</u> and recognition of repeated patterns in the accompaniment and melody. This knowledge provides significant help in reading music, learning pieces and memorizing.

Systematic review of the various learning elements is provided by a planned variety of key signatures, time signatures, tempos and musical styles. This enhances the educational appeal and provides a series of modest challenges to the student.

The damper pedal is presented in two phases. At first, simple down-up pedal style is used. Later, the legato (or syncopated) pedal is introduced.

A <u>minimum of finger numbers</u> is used. Various changed and extended hand positions are used to avoid becoming locked into a rigid five-finger position.

A reference page, correlating notes and keyboard position along with basic musical symbols, is found on the front inside cover and continued on page 46. A <u>music dictionary</u>, appropriate for level two, is provided on pages 46-47. The <u>index</u> on page 48 helps to locate explanations contained within the method.

MUSICIANSHIP CURRICULUM

Sound musicianship is attained by thorough musical study, and staying on each level until it is mastered. It is intended that this method book be part of a systematic approach to learning to play the piano. This is done by working in four books at the same level before moving up to the next level.   **1. Method   2. Theory   3. Technic   4. Repertoire**

This 4-book curriculum may be tailored to each individual student, depending upon age, ability and interests. Here are the Schaum supplements available at this level. At least one book should be assigned in each category, with preference to the first title in each group:

THEORY Books: THEORY WORKBOOK, Level 2 (see back inside cover)
                  RHYTHM WORKBOOK, Level 2
                  SCALE SPELLER

TECHNIC Books: FINGERPOWER, Level 2
                  CZERNY IN ALL KEYS, Book 1
                  TECHNIC TUNES, Book 2

REPERTOIRE Books: CLASSIC THEMES, Book 1
                  CHRISTMAS SOLOS, Level 2
                  EASY BOOGIE, Book 1
                  RHYTHM and BLUES, Book 1
                  STEPHEN FOSTER FAVORITES

SHEET MUSIC May Also Be Used For REPERTOIRE.

Optional Book Featuring CHORD SYMBOLS and IMPROVISING:
                  EASY KEYBOARD HARMONY, Book 1

(All Books are Published by Schaum Publications, Inc.)

Suggested sheet music solos are listed on the bottom of page 48.

CONTENTS

Music Reading Check List

Before playing a piece of music, old or new, check for:

1. **CLEF SIGNS.** Are they the usual treble and bass?
   Are *both hands* in the treble clef ?
   Are *both hands* in the bass clef ?

   Are there any **changes of clef** in the piece?
   You may want to mark the locations with a pencil.

2. **KEY SIGNATURE.** Keep in mind as you play:
   What notes are to be sharp or flat in the piece?
   Are there any **changes of key signature**? You may
   want to mark the locations with a pencil.

3. **TIME SIGNATURE.** Keep in mind as you play:
   How many counts in each measure?
   (UPPER number of time signature)
   What kind of note gets one count ?
   (LOWER number of time signature)

4. **MUSICAL FORM, PATTERNS and CHORDS.**

   If the form is labeled, find the passages that are the
   same or similar, for example A and A¹ .

   Look for patterns and chords in the accompaniment
   that are repeated. Also look for repeated patterns in the
   melody. You may want to mark these with a pencil.

The Metronome

Recommended Use. The metronome is a device to
determine the speed or tempo of a piece of music. Having your own metronome for home practice is not a
necessity, but it can have several benefits. It may be
helpful in developing the feeling for a steady beat, and in
learning new time signatures and new rhythms. It provides a guide to pace your practicing as you gradually
increase your speed, and also serves as an incentive to
play a piece at its intended performance tempo.

You should not become dependent upon the metronome by using it too much. Your teacher can advise
you on its proper use. Your goal should be to establish
the feeling for a steady beat within your own mind and
body, without the need of a metronome. A metronome
may be helpful in meeting this goal, as long as it is NOT
used constantly when you practice. If you are doubtful
about maintaining a steady beat, the metronome will
help show any irregularities.

For many of the pieces in this book, the directions
indicate a very slow "practice speed" setting of the
metronome at first. This can be gradually increased until
the "performance speed" (printed after the tempo mark)
is attained. Use the metronome for a few measures to
get a feeling for the tempo you want, then turn it off
and practice without it.

Metronome Markings. The original mechanical metronome was developed during the early 1800's. Although
there were several competing designs, the one marketed
by J.N. Maelzel became the most popular. The initials
"M.M.," meaning Maelzel's Metronome, are often part of
the tempo marking. However, the M.M. is optional and
is omitted in many editions.

All metronome indications include a note, an equals
sign, and one or two numbers. The number indicates
the **beats per minute**. For example, a metronome set at
60 will make 60 clicks per minute. The note shown gets
one click and usually, but not always, gets one count in
the time signature. Metronome markings in this book
use the eighth note, quarter note, and dotted quarter. Different music may use other notes.

The number represents the composer's or arrang-
er's preference for the performance speed. Two numbers indicate a range of recommended tempo, the
slowest to the fastest. You may, of course, use any
tempo between the two numbers shown. This is a
matter of personal choice.

Unless you are playing in a contest or audition, the
metronome speed is advisory and not mandatory. However, consult with your teacher if you think a different
tempo is more suitable.

Operation and Care. Metronomes come in many
shapes and sizes with varying technology. The original
and most familiar metronome is pyramid-shaped with a
swinging compound pendulum. Its mechanism is powered by a spring, and wound with a knob on the
side. An adjustable weight, which slides up and down
the pendulum, determines the speed. The tempo is
shown by the number immediately ABOVE the top edge
of the sliding weight. As the spring unwinds and loses
power, the pendulum becomes slower and eventually
stops. A flat and level surface is needed for the accuracy
of a mechanical metronome. A more expensive unit may
have a device which rings a bell with every 2nd, 3rd,
4th or 6th click. This helps to determine the first beat of
a measure with various time signatures. Unless your
teacher recommends the bell device, it is usually not
worth the added cost.

Some metronomes are powered by a motor which
must be plugged into an electric outlet. They are generally box-shaped with a dial and movable pointer to set
the tempo. As an extra-cost option, there is a small light
which can be set to flash with or without the
click. Electric metronomes are generally more accurate
and keep a consistent speed no matter how long they
are used.

The newest metronomes are electronic, ranging in
size from a box of "jello" to a credit-card. Since all
require a battery, it is preferable to choose one with an
easy-to-change, common battery size, such as the stan-
dard 9-volt. The best ones are regulated by a quartz
crystal (used in most wrist watches) and are highly
accurate. Electronic metronomes usually have both click
and flashing light. These small metronomes are desirable
because of their size and reliability. Pricey models have
an earphone jack, and may also incorporate a beep
sound with every 2nd, 3rd, 4th or 6th click.

All but the smallest metronomes list tempo marks
such as Largo, Andante, Moderato, Allegro, etc., along
with the numbers. The range of numbers associated
with each of these tempo marks is arbitrary, and differs
from one manufacturer to another. Therefore, the metronome speed numbers and tempo marks used by some
composers and arrangers may not necessarily agree with
the tempo mark labeled on the metronome.

All metronomes should be handled and placed
carefully to avoid bumps and falls. They should be kept
out of reach of small children. Older children should be
taught to handle them with care and respect — they are
NOT to be used as a toy. The mechanism of a wind-up
metronome may become damaged if wound too tight-
ly. Electric and battery powered units must be turned
off when not in use. Although most batteries will last
for one year or more, the battery should be inspected
every three months for leakage. Electric and battery
units should be kept from extremes of heat, cold and
humidity, particularly avoiding radiators, direct sunlight,
freezing temperatures and any liquids.

Marking for Melody Changing Clefs

A broken line is sometimes used to indicate a melody moving from one clef to another. This is shown in the 4th measure of the piece below. The bass clef melody notes should be given a little emphasis when played, so they are equal in loudness to the treble clef melody notes.

Early One Morning   (English Folk Song)

DIRECTIONS: Notice the metronome marking following the tempo *Andante*. Refer to page 4 for an explanation.

The descending *scale of D major,* with its correct fingering, is part of the melody in the last line of music. It is indicated with a red bracket.

DUET ACCOMPANIMENT
Stem Down = Left Hand — Stem Up = Right Hand

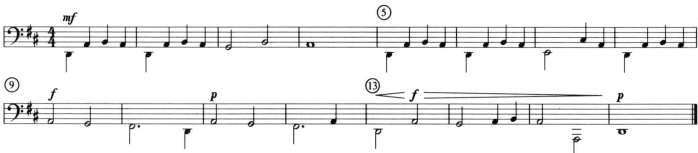

Dotted Quarter Note and Single 8th Note

A single 8th note has a curved line attached to its stem. The curved line is called a **flag.** The flag is always placed on the *right side* of the stem. See the samples to the right.

A dot placed to the right of a quarter note, increases the duration of that note by half. A dotted quarter note is often used in combination with a single 8th note. The counting is shown in the first sample measure. Notice that the rhythm is the same as when a quarter note is tied to the first of a pair of 8th notes, as in the second sample measure.

America (Carey)

DIRECTIONS: As a preparatory, count and tap the treble clef rhythm for the first line. Counting numbers have been printed in red. If you have a metronome, use it with the preparatory, starting very slowly at first so it can be done with a steady speed. This may be about 66 or slower, if necessary. Then gradually increase the setting until the performance speed is reached.

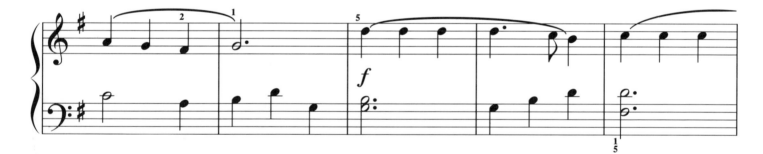

Teacher's Note: The student should say the word "and" where a plus sign (+) is written. Other abbreviations of "and" may be used, if desired. If necessary to help keep a steady beat, *all beats* may be subdivided with a plus sign. This method of counting should be used only as a remedial aid.

Dotted Quarter + 8th Note in 4/4 Time

Study the counting in the sample measure.
This same rhythm is used in the music on this page.

1   2   3   4 +

Bridal Chorus from "Lohengrin" (Wagner)

DIRECTIONS: As a preparatory, count and tap the treble clef rhythm for the first line. Counting numbers have been printed in red. If you have a metronome, use it with the preparatory, very slowly at first, as explained in the directions on page 6. Then gradually increase the setting until the performance speed is reached.

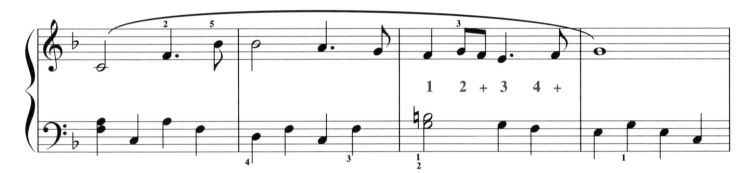

RICHARD WAGNER (VAHG-ner) 1813-1883 — Germany

Wagner is Germany's best known opera composer. He wrote a total of 13 operas. Wagner's operas gave particular attention to the total theatrical effect integrating drama, voices and music with staging. At the town of Bayreuth, he built a theater specially designed for production of his operas. It had an unusually large stage and was equipped for special effects. The orchestra played in a deep pit, designed to blend the music with the voices on stage. Annual music festivals are still performed there.

"Lohengrin" was first performed in 1850. It is a based on a medieval story of a knight with magical powers who seeks an idealistic pure love not influenced by adoration of his position. Doubt and jealousy undermine his efforts and in the end he perishes. The familiar wedding march occurs in Act 3.

Ritardando and "a tempo"

Ritardando (ree-tahr-DAHN-doh) is an Italian word meaning to <u>gradually decrease</u> the rate of speed. It is usually abbreviated by **rit**. or **ritard**.

a tempo (ah-TEHM-poh) means to return to the previous tempo. It usually follows *rit*.

Largo from "New World Symphony" (Dvorak)

DIRECTIONS: When learning a longer piece like this, it is helpful to know its musical form, since there is some repetition. The form, outlined as **A - B - C - A**, is indicated with red brackets.

The **A** section at the end is an exact repetition of the **A** at the beginning. Notice that the **B** section consists of the same four measures played twice. Look for the use of *rit*. and *a tempo* in measures 25, 27 and 33.

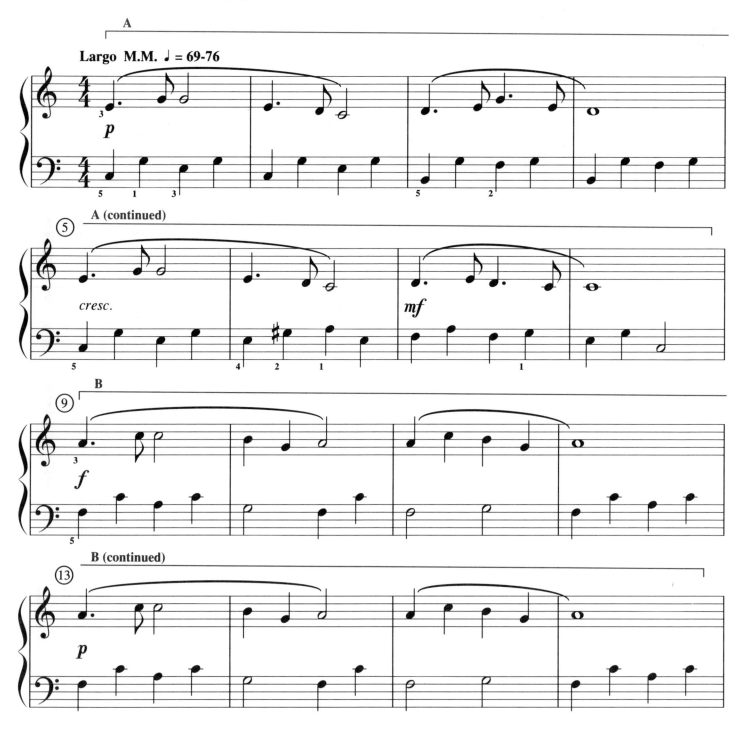

DUET ACCOMPANIMENT

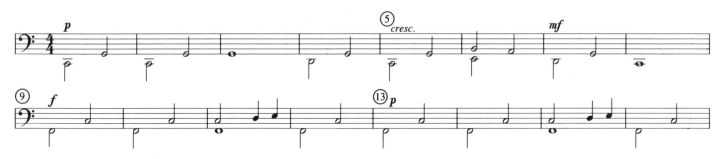

DUET ACCOMPANIMENT

ANTONIN DVORAK (DVOR-zhock) 1841-1904 — Bohemia (now part of Czechoslovakia)
Dvorak is Czechoslovakia's most famous composer. He is indebted to Johannes Brahms, the famous German composer, who encouraged his work and promoted his music. Dvorak's most popular works are the "New World Symphony" and a collection of "Slavonic Dances." In addition he wrote eight other symphonies, symphonic poems, chamber music, and numerous vocal, choral and piano works.

Between 1892 and 1895, Dvorak spent 2½ years in the United States. During that time he was director of the National Conservatory of Music in New York and composed the "New World Symphony." One of the highlights of his visit was the premiere of this symphony in New York's Carnegie Hall in December of 1893, where it was received with great enthusiasm. *Largo* is the principal theme of the second movement of that symphony.

10

Eighth Rest

Study the counting in the sample measures.
This same rhythm is used in the music on this page.

Musetta's Waltz from "La Boheme" (Puccini)

DIRECTIONS: As a preparatory, count and tap the treble clef rhythm for the first six measures,
using the right hand. Counting numbers have been printed in red. Then, tap the rhythm for both clefs,
using the left hand for the bass clef rhythm. <u>Watch for the new treble note "F" in the last line of music.</u>

GIACOMO PUCCINI (poo-CHEE-nee) 1858-1924 — Italy

Puccini came from a long tradition of father-to-son composers, started by his great-great-grandfather in the 1700's. All had lived in the northern Italian town of Lucca. Puccini's fame rests on the twelve operas written during his lifetime. The best-known are "Tosca," "La Boheme," and "Madame Butterfly." Four of his later operas were given their premiere performances at the Metropolitan Opera in New York.

"La Boheme" was first performed in 1896. It is a story of a group of Bohemians (thus the title, "La Boheme") living in the Latin quarter of Paris in the 1830's. They each earn a meager living as a painter, poet, musician and seamstress. Although one couple (Musetta and Marcello) ends up happily together, another couple (Mimi and Rudolfo) is tragically separated by Mimi's death from tuberculosis. "Musetta's Waltz" is performed in Act 2.

D.C. al Fine

D.C. al fine is an abbreviation of the Italian phrase, **da capo al fine** (dah KAH-poh ahl FEE-nay) meaning to return to the beginning and play to the word **fine**.

Da capo means "from the beginning." **Fine** means "end."

Wearing of the Green   (Irish Folk Song)

DIRECTIONS: This piece uses a 2/4 time signature. The counting of a dotted quarter and 8th note is printed in red in the fourth measure.

To play this piece, start at the beginning and play all the way to the measure where **D.C. al Fine** is printed. Without pause, continue by returning to the beginning and repeating the first eight measures. The piece ends at the double bar following the word **Fine**, in the middle of the 8th measure.

A double bar has been added in the middle of the 8th measure, just after the word **fine**, to show the end of the piece. However, this double bar does *not change the counting* for the 8th measure. As a reminder, counting numbers are printed for the second half of this measure.

Left Hand Melody — Basso Marcato

In this piece, the entire melody is in the bass clef. <u>Listen carefully as you play</u> so the treble clef accompaniment is not too loud.

Basso marcato (BAH-so mahr-KAH-toh) means to *emphasize the bass notes.*

In the accompaniment, three intervals are used to form accompaniment patterns that are repeated. These three patterns are shown in the sample measures here.

Lovely Minka   (Russian Folk Song)

DIRECTIONS: The musical form of this piece is indicated with RED. The outline is **A - A¹ - B - A¹** .
This means that the 2nd and 4th lines of music are the same.

Look up the meaning of the word **vivace** in the music dictionary on page 46.
Watch for many thumb crossings in the left hand.

This piece has two different spellings of the same black key in the bass clef. In measure 1, it is C-sharp.
In measure 3, it is D-flat. The two different spellings are said to be **enharmonic** because
they represent the same pitch in two different ways.

New Note: Treble G

The new note "G" is used near the end of this piece.
Consult the front reference page for its keyboard location.

Sweetheart Waltz from "Gypsy Baron" (Strauss)

DIRECTIONS: This piece uses **A - B - A¹ - C** form. Look for two bass patterns which are repeated many times.

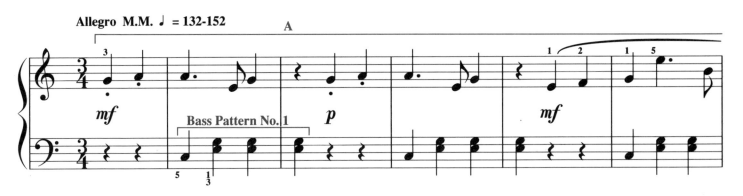

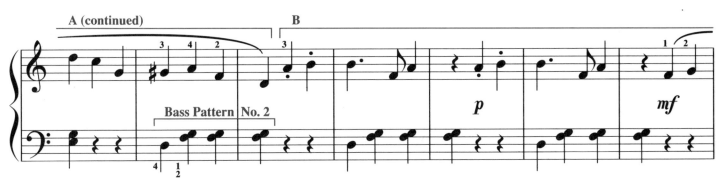

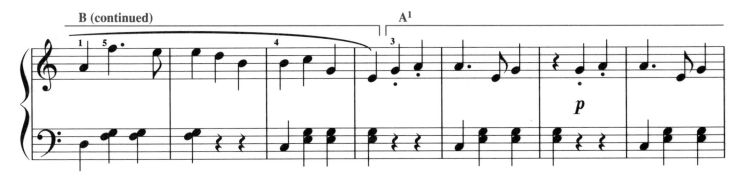

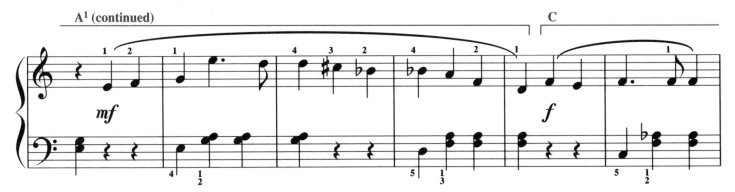

6/8 Time Signature

It is important to remember that
<u>ALL Note Values Are DOUBLED in 6/8 time:</u>

6 — SIX *counts* or *beats* in each measure.

8 — EIGHTH Note gets One Count

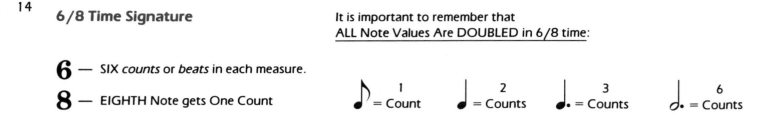

PREPARATORY: Count and tap the treble clef rhythm in the first line below, using the right hand. The counting numbers are printed in red. If you have a metronome, set it between 100 and 120 for this practice. It will help keep your counting very steady and even.

Next, count and tap the bass clef rhythm in the first line below, using the left hand. For extra practice, count and tap using both hands simultaneously (R.H. taps the treble rhythm while L.H. taps the bass rhythm). If desired, the entire piece could be done this way.

Over the River and Through the Woods (American Folk Song)

DIRECTIONS: Do the rhythmic preparatory as explained above. If necessary, add *counting numbers* to the remainder of the piece. The metronome marking is for *8th notes* because an 8th note gets one count.

Rests in 6/8 Time

Rests in 6/8 time are counted like notes
of the same value (see page 14).
Notice the dotted quarter rest.
The *whole rest* is used to fill
a *whole measure* (6 counts).

1	2	3	6
𝄽 = Count	𝄾 = Counts	𝄾• = Counts	▬ = Counts

Over the Waves   (Rosas)

DIRECTIONS: As a preparatory, count and tap the treble clef rhythm in the first line below, using the right hand.
The counting numbers are printed in red. If you have a metronome, set it between 100 and 126 for this practice.

   Next, count and tap the bass clef rhythm in the first line below, using the left hand.

Then, count and tap the rhythm using *both hands simultaneously* (same as on page 14).

JUVENTINE ROSAS (ROH-has)   1868-1894 — Mexico

   Rosas came from a family of musicians who were pure-blooded Otomi Indians. His father played harp and his brothers sang and played guitar. At age 15 he played violin in a travelling opera orchestra.

   While living in Mexico City and working at the court of the Mexican Emperor, Maximilian, Rosas wrote a very large number of waltzes, polkas and other compositions. "Over the Waves," part of a set of five waltzes, achieved extraordinary fame outside of Mexico and was mistakenly credited to Johann Strauss. This melody, which he dedicated to his sweetheart, was later adapted into a popular song titled, "The Loveliest Night of the Year."

New Note: Bass G

The new note "G" is shown in the sample staff at the right. Refer to the front reference page to find its position on the keyboard.

6/8 Time With a Fast Tempo

Usually the metronome numbers are for the note which gets one count. However, with fast tempos, other note values are used. Here the metronome numbers are for a *dotted quarter note*. This means, in this piece each metronome click gets THREE COUNTS.

When counting 6/8 time in a rapid tempo, a slight accent should be given to the 1st and 4th beats.

Soldier's Chorus from "Faust" (Gounod)

DIRECTIONS: This piece uses **A - A¹ - B - A¹** form, as shown with red brackets. This means that the final eight measures are *the same* as the second eight measures. Counting numbers have been printed in red for the first four measures.

Notice the three accompaniment patterns that are labeled with red. They occur many times throughout the piece.

B

B (continued)

cresc.

A¹

A¹ (continued)

CHARLES GOUNOD (GOO-noh) 1818-1893 — France

Gounod is best known for his opera, "Faust," although he wrote many other operas and a large amount of sacred and secular choral and vocal music. "Faust" was the most popular French opera of the 1800's. From its premiere in 1859, it was performed over 1,200 times in the city of Paris by 1902. It also achieved popularity in many other countries, especially Germany.

The legend of Faust has roots going back to medieval times. The opera is based on a story by the German poet, Goethe. It tells of an aged philosopher (Faust) who bargains with the devil (Mephistopheles) to regain his youthfulness. Faust becomes involved in a love triangle which ends tragically for all, by the diabolical meddling and manipulation of Mephistopheles. The "Soldier's Chorus" is part of Act 4.

Purpose of Scale Study

1. **Helps Finger Coordination and Technic.** Scale playing involves use of thumb under, finger cross-overs and playing on many black keys. All of this is valuable in developing the finger dexterity and coordination needed in playing many pieces. It also helps establish correct hand, finger and wrist positions.

2. **Makes Music Reading Easier.** Scale excerpts and passages occur often in music. The visual recognition of such passages makes music reading easier.

3. **Provides Valuable Ear Training.** Careful listening while playing scales helps establish an aural recognition of the major tonality.

4. **Provides Help in Transposing.** Use of scale degree numbers is one useful method of transposing.

5. **Leads to Understanding of Intervals and Chords.** A knowledge of scales is an essential element of music theory that is the basis for analysis and construction of intervals and chords.

The scales on pages 18 and 19 need NOT be learned at the same time. They may be played one at a time, along with other pieces that follow. The different scales may be used as a warm-up for pieces in the same key as the scale.

Major Scale Fingerings

On pages 18 and 19 you will find major scales, along with the fingering for each hand, ascending and descending.

Scale fingerings <u>always avoid placing the thumb or fifth finger on a black key.</u> These fingers are shorter than the other fingers making it more difficult to reach the black keys.

C Major Scale
DIRECTIONS: Practice each scale, hands separately, several times per day until it can be played easily and accurately. <u>Scale degree numbers are printed in red.</u> Finger numbers are printed in black. Take special care to play legato at places with the thumb under and where fingers cross over the thumb.

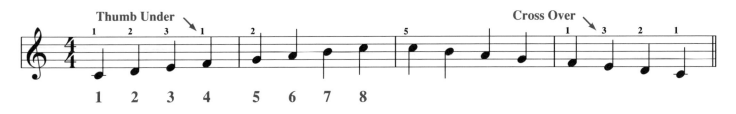

F Major Scale
DIRECTIONS: Practice each scale, hands separately, several times per day until it can be played easily and accurately. Be sure to observe the *key signature*.

The bass clef scale begins with a <u>NEW NOTE "F,"</u> below the bass staff.

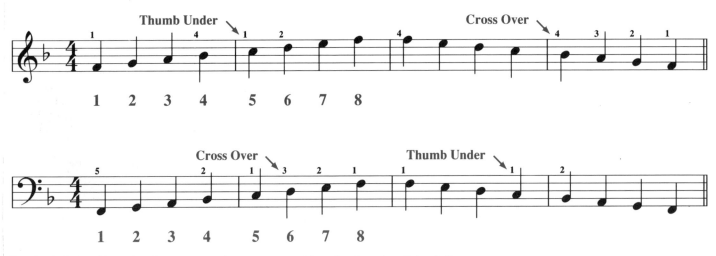

Teacher's Note: Tetrachords are purposely not presented here for the sake of simplicity. Tetrachords will be introduced with the circle of keys later in this series.

G Major Scale

DIRECTIONS: Practice each scale, hands separately, several times per day until it can be played easily and accurately. <u>Scale degree numbers are printed in red.</u> Finger numbers are printed in black. Take special care to play legato at places with the thumb under and where fingers cross over the thumb.

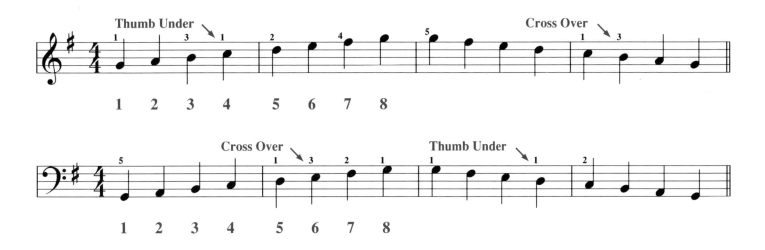

D Major Scale

DIRECTIONS: Practice each scale, hands separately, several times per day until it can be played easily and accurately. Be sure to observe the *key signature.* Watch especially for places with the thumb under and for finger cross-overs.

B-flat Major Scale

DIRECTIONS: Practice each scale, hands separately, several times per day until it can be played easily and accurately. Be sure to observe the *key signature.* Watch especially for places with the thumb under and for finger cross-overs.

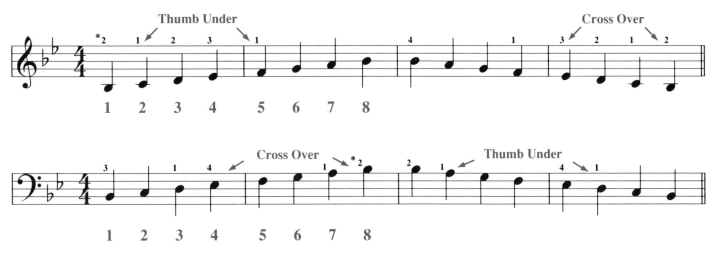

Teacher's Note: <u>The scales on pages 18 and 19 need NOT be learned at the same time.</u> They may be done individually, according to your preference, along with other pieces that follow. A scale may be used as a warm-up for pieces in the same key as the scale.

* The fingering will have to be adjusted when two or more octaves are played.

Damper Pedal Introduction

On an acoustic piano, the pedal farthest to the right is called the *damper pedal.* When pressed, it pulls the dampers (thick felt pads) away from all the piano strings, allowing them to sound freely. The damper pedal is used to blend sounds, to help achieve a legato effect, and to enhance the sound of the instrument. For electronic instruments, see the bottom of this page.

The damper pedal is pressed with the toe of your right foot. <u>Your heel should always be ON THE FLOOR.</u>

Be sure to <u>lift the pedal all the way up</u>, without lifting the heel. Don't use the pedal as a footrest, otherwise there will be a continuous blurred sound. Listen carefully as you use the pedal.

The <u>operation of the pedal should be SILENT.</u> Your foot should keep in contact with the pedal as it is used. Be careful not to let it thump on the way down or up. If the pedal squeaks or makes a clicking noise when pressed, it should be repaired by a technician.

The marking for the damper pedal, resembling a bracket, is printed below the lower staff.

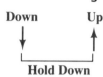

- When the pedal mark goes down, the pedal is to be pressed down with the right foot.

- The horizontal line of the pedal mark indicates that the pedal is to remain pressed down.

- When the pedal mark goes up, the pedal is to be lifted silently, all the way up. *The heel must remain on the floor.*

The movement of the pedal should be precisely coordinated with the notes directly above the start and end of the pedal mark. In the second measure of the preparatory below, press down the pedal at exactly the same time as you play the notes on the 4th beat. The pedal is to remain down until you play the notes on the 1st beat of the next measure. Lift the pedal at the same time as you play the notes on the 1st beat.

DIRECTIONS: This preparatory is the 2nd and 3rd lines of the piece on page 21. Practice it several times a day until it can be played easily and accurately. Notice that the pedal mark at the end of the 1st line is continued in the 2nd line.

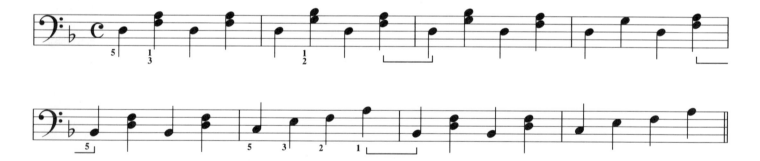

DIRECTIONS: This preparatory is the first eight measures of the piece on page 22. Practice it several times a day until it can be played easily and accurately. The pedal mark at the end of the 1st line is continued in the 2nd line.

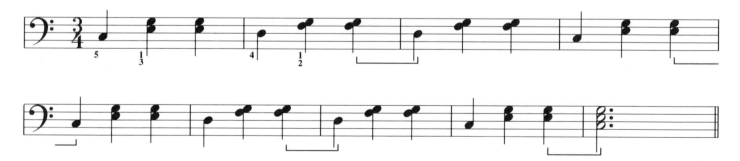

Pedals on Electronic Instruments

On a full size digital piano there are usually two pedals. The pedal on the *right* functions the same as the damper pedal on an acoustic piano.

On a portable electronic piano or keyboard the pedal may be an optional accessory, plugged into the back of the instrument. There are sometimes two different kinds of pedals available. A "sustain pedal" operates the same as a damper pedal. An "expression pedal" or "volume pedal" controls the loudness and is *not the same* as a damper pedal.

Damper Pedal Usage

In this piece, the pedal always goes DOWN on the 4th beat and UP on the 1st beat. This is done for sake of simplicity because this is the first piece of music with damper pedal. Later pieces will have other rhythms associated with the pedal patterns. Pedal patterns may be of differing length and rhythm within the same piece.

Hatikvah (Song of Hope) (Cohen)*

DIRECTIONS: Learn to play the notes and correct rhythm first. Then, before adding the pedal, play the first preparatory exercise shown on page 20. For extra work, play the entire piece using just left hand and pedal.

This piece is in the key of d minor. D minor is related to the key of F major because both have the same key signature. This piece uses A - A - B - C form, as shown with red brackets. Two broken chords are used many times in this piece. They are labeled in red as "Dm" (d minor) and "Gm" (g minor).

The bass pattern in the 2nd measure of the **B** section occurs two other times. Look for them.

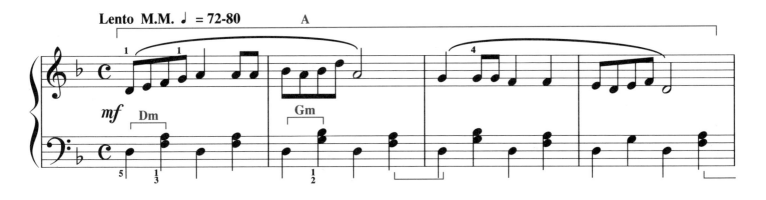

* "Hatikvah" (hah-TICK-vah) was composed about 1882 by Samuel Cohen and is based on a Romanian folk song. It soon became the anthem of the Zionist movement and since 1948 has been the national anthem of Israel.

Repeat Sign   Two dots in the center of the staff, next to a double bar are called a *repeat sign*. A repeated section is played <u>one extra time</u>. When finished with the repeat, continue the remainder of the piece without interruption. There may be any number of measures in a repeated section. The repeat marks are often omitted at the beginning of a piece.

Santa Lucia (Italian Folk Song) DIRECTIONS: Learn the notes and correct rhythm first, then add pedal. As a pedal preparatory, play the 2nd exercise shown on page 20. This piece uses **A - A - B - B¹** form. The repeated section is part of this form. The broken chords labeled "C Pattern," "G7 Pattern" and "F Pattern" are used many times.

Syncopation   The rhythm created by the tied melody notes in measures 12-13-14 is a form of syncopation. Syncopation (sink-uh-PAY-shun) is a rhythmical shift away from the normal pulse. In 3/4 time there is normally a slight pulse on the first beat of every measure. The tied notes shift this pulse to the 2nd beat in measures 13 and 14.

New Leger Note: Treble A   The new note "A" is on a leger line above the treble staff, in measure 10. See the front reference page for its keyboard position.

Siciliano from "Flute Sonata No. 2"   (Bach)

DIRECTIONS: Learn the notes and correct rhythm first, then add the pedal.
For a pedal preparatory, play the left hand with the pedal for the entire piece.

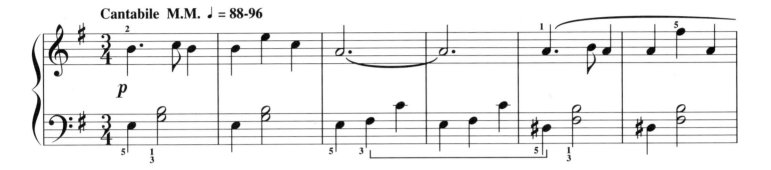

JOHANN SEBASTIAN BACH (BAHKH) 1685-1750 — Germany

Bach, one of the most famous musicians of all time, composed a very large amount of music, enough to fill 45 oversized encyclopedia-thick volumes. Most of his music was written by necessity. He was employed as a church musician and also as music director for several noble families that expected new music for their private religious services, along with music for numerous special occasions and receptions given by the family. Bach was not able to go to the nearest music store and pick out what he needed. Music stores, as we know them, did not exist, and there were few music publishers. Bach had to write the music he needed.

The "Siciliano," named for a dance from Sicily, is the second movement of Bach's "Flute Sonata No. 2," written in 1717.

Key Signature: E-flat Major

The *three flats* used in the key signature for *E-flat Major* mean that all B's, E's and A's are flat.

A key signature eliminates the need to write a flat sign for every B, E and A.

Vilia from "The Merry Widow" (Lehar)

DIRECTIONS: Be sure to play all B's, E's and A's *flat* as indicated in the key signature.
Watch the finger numbers carefully, especially for the black keys. Be aware of the 2/4 time signature.

The first four measures of accompaniment contain variations of the same E-flat chord. This will be helpful in learning the left hand part. The musical form is **A - B - A - B¹** . Each line of music represents one section of the form.

FRANZ LEHAR (LEH-har) 1870-1948 —Hungary

Although born in Hungary, Lehar is often considered an Austrian composer because he spent his adult life in Austria. He started his career as a military band director. Between 1901 and 1934 he composed the music for 38 operettas. "The Merry Widow," written in 1905, remains the best known. It was extremely successful and has been played in many countries throughout the world. It was performed over 1,000 times in the United States.

The story of "The Merry Widow" is set in Paris in the early 1900's and involves flirtations and intrigues of diplomatic officials and their wives. "Vilia" is sung during the second act.

Cradle Song (Wiegenlied) (Schubert, D-498)

DIRECTIONS: This piece is in the key of E-flat major (see page 24). Watch the finger numbers carefully, especially for the black keys.

Two chord patterns occur many times in the accompaniment. They are shown with red brackets.
The musical form is **A - A¹ - B - A¹** . Each line of music represents one letter of the form.

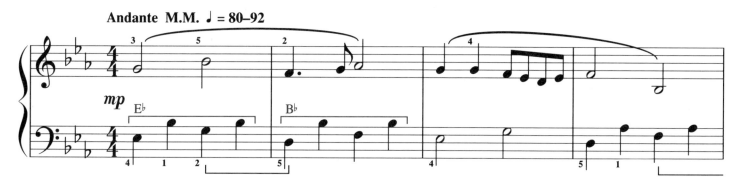

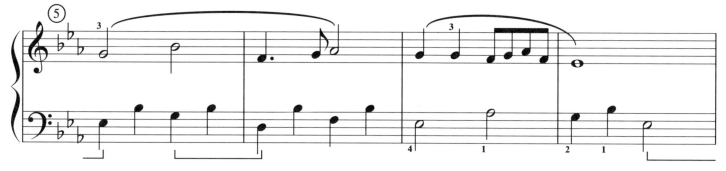

DUET ACCOMPANIMENT
Stem Down = Left Hand — Stem Up = Right Hand

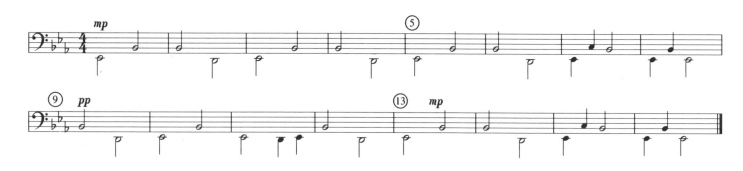

Repeat with 1st and 2nd Endings

The brackets numbered **1.** and **2.**, at the end of a repeated section, are called *first and second endings*.

When playing the *first time* through a repeated section, the measure under the number **1.** bracket is played. During the *second time* through, skip the measure with the number **1.** and play measure number **2.** instead. After the 2nd ending, continue playing until the end of the piece.

There is to be no hesitation or interruption of the rhythm when playing the first and second endings. 1st and 2nd endings may be one or more measures long and may occur anywhere in the middle of a piece or at the end of a piece.

Before playing a piece, check to see if there are any repeat signs. If so, study each page to see where the repeated sections begin and end. In this piece, there are two separate repeated sections, one on each page. Each repeat is to be treated individually. On page 27, after playing the first ending, go back to the beginning of the repeated section in the *same line of music* (do NOT go back to the beginning on page 26).

Barcarolle from "Tales of Hoffmann" (Offenbach)

DIRECTIONS: This piece is in the key of D Major. This means all F's and C's are sharp. See page 14 for an explanation of the 6/8 time signature. The metronome marking is for *8th notes,* because an 8th note gets one count.

The accompaniment patterns shown with a red bracket occur many times throughout the piece. The pedal mark in the first measure and also on page 27, in the first measure of line 2, is used only *after the first ending* in both places.

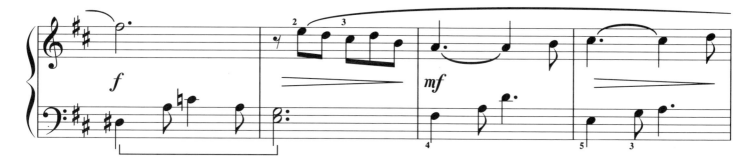

JACQUES OFFENBACH (OFF-fen-bahk)   1819-1880 — France (Germany)

Although born in Germany, Offenbach is usually considered to be a French composer because he spent most of his life in France. Offenbach is best known for his many operettas with light-hearted and sometimes frivolous plots. "Tales of Hoffmann," however, is his only opera and is more serious in nature.

Hoffmann is a poetry student who tells his college friends of his three romances. Each act of the opera is a different episode. The *Barcarolle* is at the beginning of the third act, an evening scene in Venice aside the grand canal. The music is a love song imitating the swaying rhythm of gondolas being pushed through the water. It was first performed in 1881.

Key Signature: A Major

The *three sharps* used in the key signature for *A Major* mean that all F's, C's and G's are sharp.

A key signature eliminates the need to write a sharp sign for every F, C and G in the piece.

Cherokee Corn Legend (Native American)

DIRECTIONS: An A major triad is used in the 1st and 2nd measures, first as a blocked chord, then as a broken chord. Similar use of the E7 chord (5th omitted) is found in the 3rd and 4th measures. These A and E7 chords recur later in the music. Look for the new note "E" on a leger line above the bass staff, in the first measure (see page 29).

The musical form is **A - B - A - B¹** . Each line of music represents one letter of the form.

Listen for the surprise change from major to minor in the final measure.

Andantino M.M. ♩ = 96-104

NATIVE AMERICAN MUSIC —Like most folk music, native American music evolved as it was passed on by memory from one generation to another. This melody is an authentic Cherokee tribal theme collected and transcribed by Harvey Worthington Loomis. According to legend, on warm summer nights, the corn grew so fast that you could hear the ears crackle as they unfolded. This phenomenon was called the "walker in the night."

Bass Leger Notes: D, E and F

This piece uses three leger notes above the bass staff. The note **F** is new. See the front reference page for the keyboard positions.

D   E   F

Bonnie Laddie, Highland Laddie (Scotch Folk Song)

DIRECTIONS: Be sure to play all F's, C's and G's *sharp* as indicated in the key signature. Watch the finger numbers carefully, especially for the black keys.

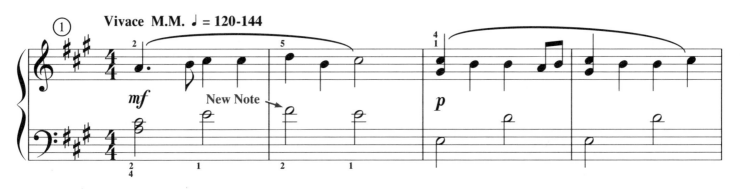

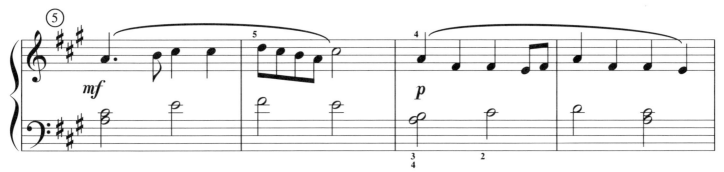

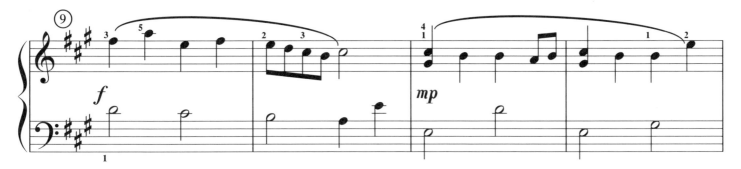

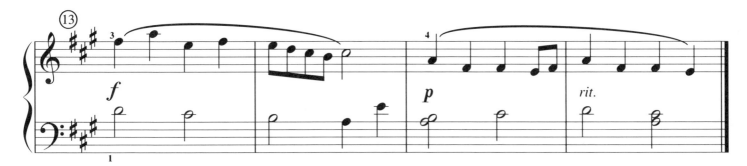

DUET ACCOMPANIMENT

Where ha'e ye been a' the day, Bonnie laddie, Highland laddie?
Saw ye him that's far away, Bonnie laddie, Highland laddie,
On his head a bonnet blue, Bonnie laddie, Highland laddie,
Tartan plaid and Highland trew, Bonnie laddie, Highland laddie.

3/8 Time Signature

3 — THREE *counts* or *beats* in each measure.

8 — EIGHTH Note gets One Count

♪ = Count ¹   ♩ = Counts ²   ♩. = Counts ³

Waltz of the Flowers from "The Nutcracker" (Tchaikowsky)

DIRECTIONS: The note values here are the same as in 6/8 time (see page 14). The counting has been printed in red in two measures. The metronome marking is for *8th notes* because an 8th note gets one count.

Learn to play the notes and correct rhythm first. Then, before adding the pedal, play the entire piece using left hand and pedal. The musical form is **A - B - A - C.** Each line of music represents one letter of the form.

Allegro M.M. ♪ = 120-138

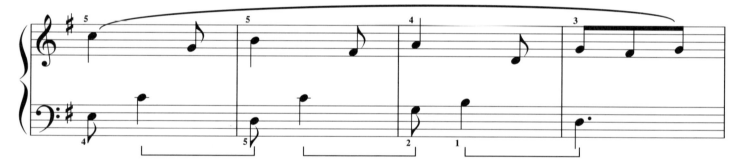

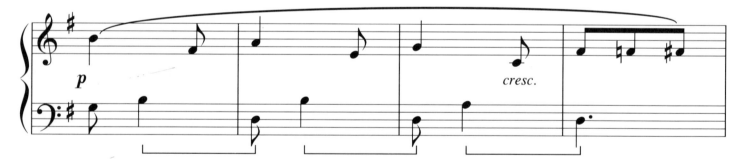

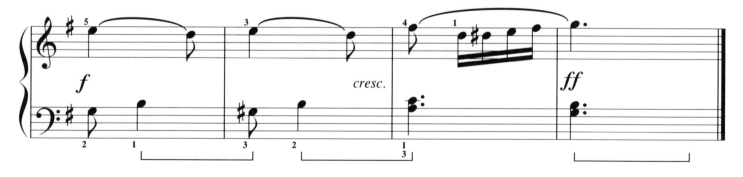

PETER I. TCHAIKOWSKY (chy-CUFF-skee) 1840-1893 — Russia

"The Nutcracker" is a full length ballet telling a story of a girl who dreams that her toys come to life under the Christmas tree. It was first performed in St. Petersburg, Russia, in 1892. Many American ballet companies currently produce this ballet during the Christmas season. Eight excerpts from the ballet form the "Nutcracker Suite," Tchaikowsky's most popular work. The music was included in a classic animated film by Walt Disney titled "Fantasia," now available on videotape.

Broken Chord Patterns

The sample line shows different broken chord patterns used on this page. Each pattern is labeled with its chord symbol. The E7 chord has two different forms. The Am and Dm patterns are used quite frequently.

The Moldau from "My Fatherland" (Smetana)

DIRECTIONS: The metronome numbers are for a *dotted quarter note*. This means in this piece <u>each metronome click gets THREE COUNTS</u>. The red asterisks show where each click will fit in the first line of music.

See page 11 for a description of **D.C. al fine**.

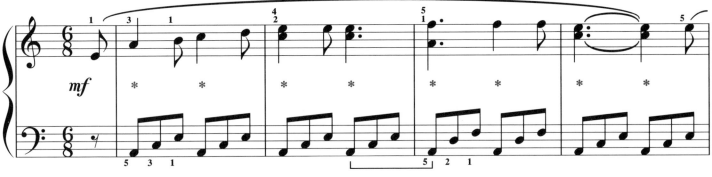

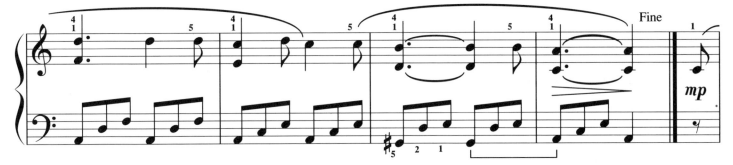

BEDRICH SMETANA (SMET-tuh-nah) 1824-1884 — Bohemia (part of Czechoslovakia)

"My Fatherland" is a symphonic poem written to honor Smetana's native country. It was first performed in Prague in 1882. The Moldau is one of the principal rivers in Bohemia. This movement of the orchestral music traces the terrain along the river as it flows through the country. A **symphonic poem** is a piece of orchestral music that describes a mood, tells a story, or provides a musical picture or panorama of a place or event.

16th Notes   TWO 16th notes are counted the same as ONE 8th note. The counting in the last sample measure has extra syllables for the subdivisions of the beat. They are to be said, "two - ee - and - ah." *

At first, 16th notes will be used in pairs or in groups of four. 16th notes have a *double beam* (the stems are joined by TWO heavy lines) as shown in the samples. The counting has been printed in red.

March from "William Tell" (Rossini)

March from "William Tell" **(Rossini)** DIRECTIONS: As a preparatory, count and tap the rhythm for the treble clef notes in the first two lines. If you have a metronome, start at a speed of 80. Notice that <u>each metronome click represents one EIGHTH NOTE</u>; therefore there will be FOUR clicks in each measure.

Watch for finger changes in the right hand on the repeated notes. This makes it easier to play in a fast tempo.

* Teacher's Note: You may prefer another way of subdividing the counts of the 16th notes. Four syllable words, such as "Mis-sis-sip-pi," or "Chat-ta-noo-ga" are possibilities.

The metronome setting for 8th notes is for practice and rhythmic training. For a finished performance the metronome may be converted to a quarter note setting to conform with the time signature.

More 16th Notes

The rhythms on this page are a little different than those on page 32. Counting numbers have been printed in red.

Sourwood Mountain (American Mountain Tune)

DIRECTIONS: This piece is in the key of E-flat major. Be sure to play all B's, E's and A's *flat* as indicated in the key signature. As a preparatory, count and tap the rhythm for the treble clef notes for the first two lines. If you have a metronome, start at a speed of 80. <u>Each metronome click represents one 8th NOTE; therefore there will be FOUR clicks in each measure (see footnote, page 32).</u> The musical form is **A - B - A - B**, each letter represented by one line of music.

DUET ACCOMPANIMENT

AMERICAN MOUNTAIN MUSIC

"Sourwood Mountain" is one of the best loved American mountain songs. Because of its popularity, there are many variations both in lyrics and melody. Sourwood Mountain is in Russell County, Virginia, although the tune is also said to be from Kentucky. The music is often used by fiddlers for country dancing. It is a whimsical love song with many nonsense syllables in the lyrics.

34

Legato Pedal

The pedal mark shown in the sample measure is called the **legato pedal** or *syncopated pedal*. The toe does a quick up-and-down movement at the same time as the notes are played on the first beat of each measure. This allows one measure to blend smoothly into another, thus the name *legato pedal*.

Be careful, the pedal must come UP at exactly the same time as the hands play the notes on the first beat. The pedal is IMMEDIATELY LOWERED to minimize interruption of the sound. The quick up-down foot movement resembles a "hiccup." This pattern of changing the pedal on the first count is very common in 3/8 and 3/4 time.

Another use for the legato pedal is to avoid blurring of one note or chord into another. In this case, pedal changes can occur with *any note* and on *any beat* in a measure. For the sake of simplicity, all pedal changes occur on the first beat on pages 34 and 35.

Sidewalks of New York (Lawlor and Blake)

DIRECTIONS: Learn to play the notes and correct rhythm first. Then, before adding the pedal, play the entire piece using left hand and pedal. Use a much slower metronome speed when first adding the pedal.

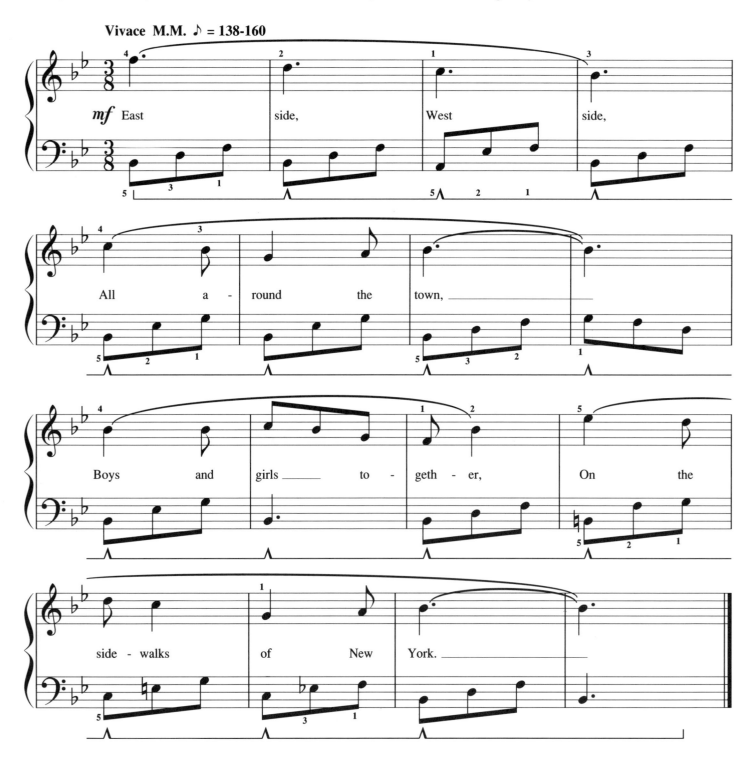

The Story of the Rose ("Heart of My Heart") (Andrew Mack)

DIRECTIONS: Learn to play the notes and correct rhythm first. Then, before adding the pedal, play the entire piece using left hand and pedal. Use a much slower metronome speed when first adding the pedal.

This piece has the same key signature and time signature as the one on page 34. Many of the accompaniment patterns are also the same. The bass clef part in the last line of music is the same on both pages.

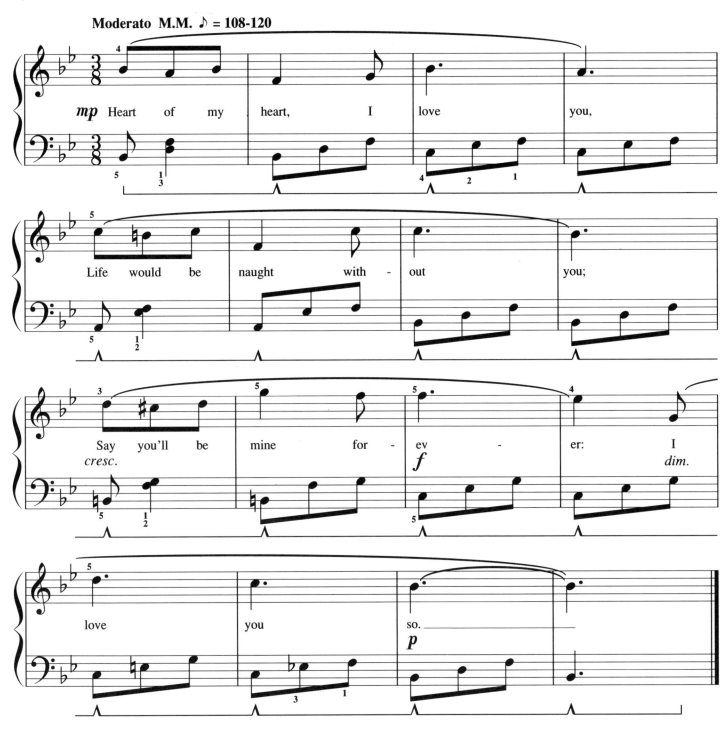

Moderato M.M. ♪ = 108-120

mp Heart of my heart, I love you,

Life would be naught with - out you;

Say you'll be mine for - ev - er: I
cresc. *f* *dim.*

love you so. *p*

GAY NINETIES MUSIC —

The pieces on pages 34 and 35 were written and published in New York during the 1890's. Both composers were also well-known performers. Live music in theaters, dance halls and cabarets reigned supreme during that period.

During the 1890's, radio and TV along with stereos, cassettes and CD's did not exist. Use of electricity in the home was pretty much limited to lighting. Record players of the time were powered by a large coil spring, wound with a hand crank. The disk and cylinder recordings were expensive and of poor sound quality. The closest things to a juke box were bulky coin-operated mechanical music boxes and player-pianos. The player-piano, with its interchangeable perforated rolls, was gaining a place in the home as mechanical improvements were made.

It was common for many households to have a piano or parlor organ. The organ was powered by bellows operated with foot pedals, sometimes called a *pump organ*. For recreation, families often gathered around the instrument to sing along. Sheet music was in great demand. As a result, most major cities of the time had several local publishers of music.

The music on this page may be combined with the piece on page 34 to form a medley. A **medley** is a group of two or more pieces or musical excerpts played in succession to form a single unit. Play page 35 first, then continue by going back and playing page 34 without pause or interruption. The medley will sound better if the piece with the faster tempo is played last.

16th Notes in 3/4 Time

If necessary, refer to pages 32-33 for an explanation of 16th note counting. Counting numbers have been printed in red.

Ay, Ay, Ay (Spanish Creole Folk Song)

DIRECTIONS: This piece is in the key of C major which has NO sharps or flats in the key signature.

As a preparatory, count and tap the rhythm for the treble clef notes for the first and third lines of music. If you have a metronome, start at a speed of 100 or slower. Each metronome click represents one EIGHTH NOTE; therefore there will be SIX clicks in each measure.

The musical form is **A - A - B - A**. Each line of music represents one letter of the form.

* **Teacher's Note:** The metronome setting for 8th notes is for practice, and to promote a more accurate feeling for the rhythm. For a finished performance the metronome may be converted to a quarter note setting to conform with the time signature.

Change of Clef   The *extra clef sign* at the end of the second line of music is an advance notice that the left hand will be playing *treble clef* notes in the next line. For the rest of the piece, <u>both hands will be playing in treble clef.</u>

Syncopation   The rhythm of the note group **8th** + **dotted quarter** is a common form of *syncopation* (see page 23). This rhythm is labeled with red brackets in the first line of music.

Listen To The Mocking Bird (Winner)*

DIRECTIONS: As a preparatory, count and tap the rhythm for the treble clef notes for the first three lines of music, preferably with metronome. Set the metronome at about 88 to start. <u>Each metronome click represents one 8th NOTE</u>; therefore there will be EIGHT clicks in each measure. Four broken chord patterns are shown with red. The C chord pattern has two forms: an inversion and root position.

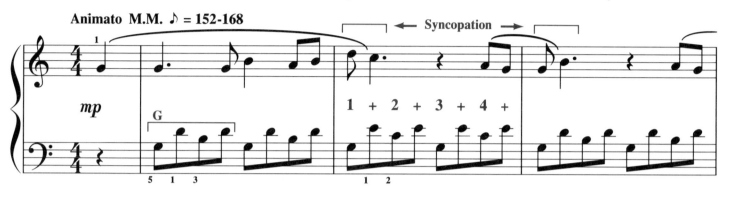

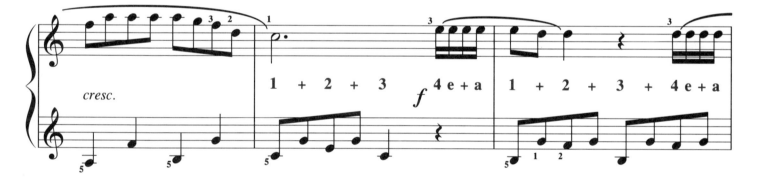

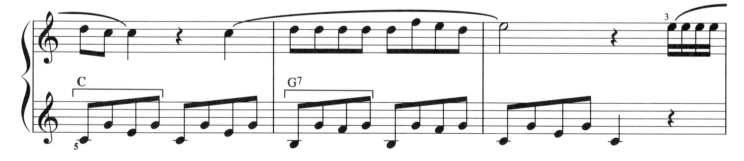

* Septimus Winner (1827-1902) was a Philadelphia music teacher and composer. For this piece he used the pseudonym, Alice Hawthorne, to honor his mother. "Listen to the Mocking Bird," written in 1854, sold 20 million copies during the composer's lifetime.

More Syncopation   The rhythm of the note group, **eighth-quarter-eighth**, is a very common form of syncopation. It is extremely important that you learn the correct rhythm and train your eye to recognize this note group.

Another common form of syncopation occurs between the 3rd and 4th sample measures.
The clue is the tie which crosses the bar line.

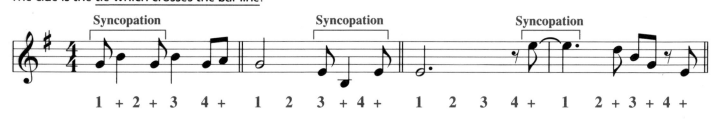

Sometimes I Feel Like a Motherless Child (African American Spiritual)

DIRECTIONS: As a rhythmic preparatory, count and tap the treble clef rhythm for the first two lines of music, preferably with a metronome. Set the metronome at about 52 to start. Each metronome click represents one QUARTER NOTE; therefore there will be FOUR clicks in each measure. Counting numbers are printed in red.

The pedal should be added only after the notes and rhythm can be played correctly and confidently. As a pedal preparatory, play the left hand with the pedal for the entire piece. Notice that there is a change of pedal on the 1st and 3rd beat of every measure. This is a common rhythm pattern for the legato pedal in 4/4 time.

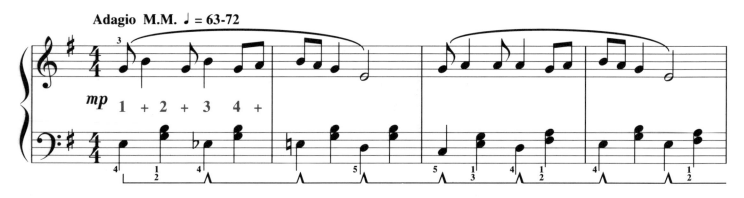

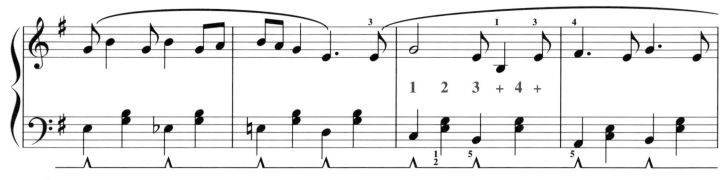

Review of Syncopation   It is very important to:

1. **Recognize the note groups on sight** in the music.
2. **Play the correct rhythm.**

The counting will differ, depending upon which beat the syncopation appears. The note groups are indicated with red brackets.

John Henry (American Folk Ballad) DIRECTIONS: As a rhythmic preparatory, count and tap the treble clef rhythm for the entire piece, preferably with a metronome. Set the metronome at about 80 to start. <u>Each metronome click represents one QUARTER NOTE</u>; therefore there will be FOUR clicks in each measure.

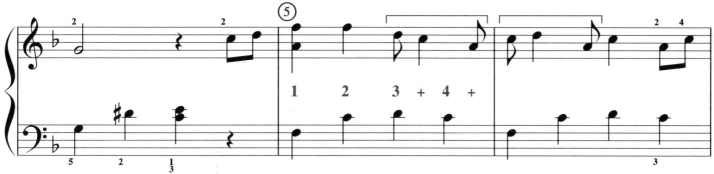

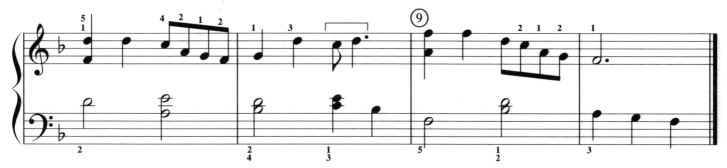

DUET ACCOMPANIMENT

STORY of JOHN HENRY

John Henry is a folk hero, probably an African American, one of hundreds of men who worked to blast a tunnel through the mountains of West Virginia for the Chesapeake and Ohio railroad in the early 1870's. His job was a "steel driver," one who repeatedly strikes a long steel drill with a sledge hammer to slowly bore a hole through rock for implanting explosives. Work shifts were commonly ten hours long.

The story is intertwined with fact and fantasy and has many variations. A mechanical drill powered by a steam engine prompted a contest between man and machine. John Henry, a champion steel-driver, was the logical choice. During the contest, he bored two 7-foot holes, but the steam drill bored only one 9-foot hole. John Henry supposedly died of exhaustion after the contest.

A **ballad** is a sentimental or romantic song which tells a story, often with descriptive music and several verses. The versions of "John Henry" range from 4 to 19 verses.

40

Pomp and Circumstance (Elgar, Op. 39 No. 1)

DIRECTIONS: This piece is in the key of A major (see page 28). Be sure to play all F's, C's and G's sharp.

Several measures have syncopated patterns. Counting for the first pattern is printed in red.

The *1st ending* begins with the last measure of the second line of music and is continued in the third line. At the repeat sign, go back to the beginning of the piece. 1st and 2nd endings are explained on pages 26 and 27.

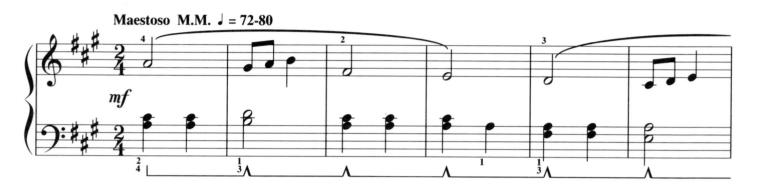

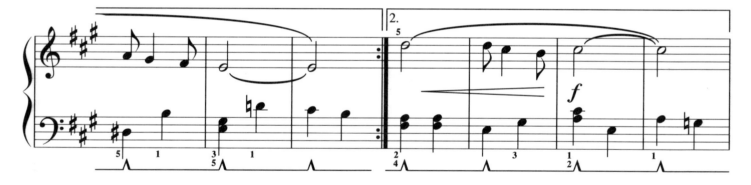

EDWARD ELGAR (ELL-gar)   1857-1934 — England

The excerpt on this page is Elgar's most famous theme. You will probably recognize it as often played at high school graduation ceremonies. It is an orchestral piece written in 1901. In 1911, the same theme was recycled for the coronation of King Edward VII of England and given the title "Land of Hope and Glory."

During Elgar's visits to the United States, he received an honorary degree from Yale University in 1904, and from the University of Pittsburgh in 1907. He also received many honors in his own country, where his music is better known. He composed numerous works for orchestra, chorus, vocal solo and chamber groups.

Left Hand Melody — Melodia Marcato

In this piece, part of the melody is in the bass clef. Listen carefully as you play so the treble clef accompaniment is not too loud.

Basso marcato (BAH-so   mahr-KAH-toh) means to *emphasize the bass notes.*

Melodia marcato (mell-OH-dee-ah   mahr-KAH-toh) means to *emphasize the melody notes,* usually in the treble.

Oh Susanna (Foster)

DIRECTIONS: The musical form is **A - A¹ - B - A¹** . Each line of music represents one letter of the form.

Look for two intervals in the treble clef; they are used frequently for accompaniment.

STEPHEN FOSTER (FOSS-ter)   1826-1864 — United States

Stephen Foster was born in a small town near Pittsburgh, Pennsylvania. He was almost entirely self-trained as a composer.

"Oh Susanna" was first performed in 1847 and established his reputation as a songwriter. Foster's songs are about the southern United States. The lyrics for many of them use African American dialect. The effectiveness and popularity of his songs are remarkable because he lived entirely in the north, except for one short visit to the southern states. Of the nearly 200 songs he wrote, about a dozen remain well known.

Long after his death, Foster was honored by being the first American musician elected to the Hall of Fame at New York University. His manuscripts and papers are preserved at Foster Hall at the University of Pittsburgh. A memorial to Stephen Foster is located in northern Florida on the Suwannee River (Foster spelled it Swanee), immortalized in his song, "Old Folks At Home."   It is the official state song for Florida. Foster's "My Old Kentucky Home" is Kentucky's official state song.

16th Notes in 3/8 Time

TWO 16th notes are counted the same as ONE 8th note in 3/8 time. Counting numbers have been printed in red.

Change of Key Signature

This piece *changes the key signature* in the last two lines. At the end of the second line of music, as an advance notice, there is a *natural sign* in each staff to cancel the previous key signature of one flat, followed by a new key signature of one sharp.

Transposition

The melody and accompaniment in the last two lines are the same as in the first two lines, except everything is *transposed* from the key of F major to the key of G major.

The Ash Grove (Welsh Folk Song)

DIRECTIONS: As a preparatory, count and tap the rhythm for the treble clef notes in the first two lines. If you have a metronome, start at a speed of 66. Notice that each metronome click represents one EIGHTH NOTE.

Watch for the change of key signature at the end of the second line of music.

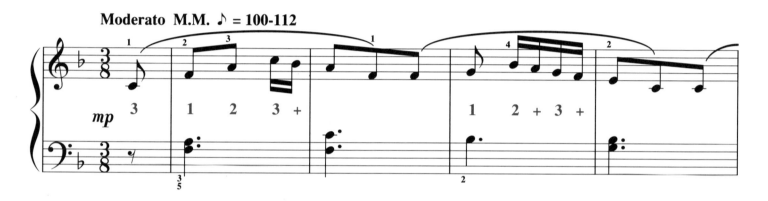

16th Notes in 6/8 Time

The counting of 16th notes in 6/8 time is the same as 3/8 time (see page 42). Counting numbers are printed in red.

Ever Free from "La Traviata" (Verdi)

DIRECTIONS: As a preparatory, count and tap the rhythm for the treble clef notes in the first two lines, preferably with a metronome, starting at a speed of about 108. <u>Each metronome click represents one EIGHTH NOTE.</u>

Learn to play the notes and correct rhythm first. Then, before adding the pedal, play the entire piece using left hand and pedal. Use a much slower metronome speed when first adding the pedal. This piece uses an irregular pedal pattern, combining legato pedal with down/up pedal styles. If necessary, review the *legato pedal* on page 34.

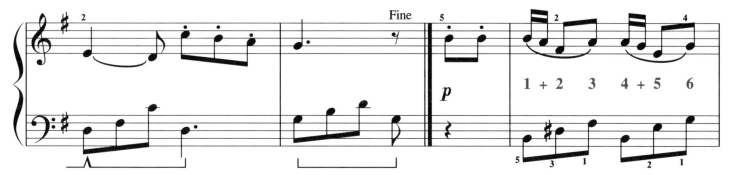

GIUSEPPI VERDI (joo-SEHP-ee VAIR-dee) 1813-1901 — Italy

Verdi is one of the best-loved of all opera composers. Most American opera companies stage at least one of his operas every season. "La Traviata" was first produced in Venice, Italy in 1853. It gradually gained in popularity and was first performed in New York City in 1856.

"La Traviata" is set in 1840's Paris. Violetta is a superficial and extravagant socialite loved by Alfredo. He is sincere and serious in his love, and conservative and provincial in manner. "Ever Free" is sung by Violetta in Act I, expressing commitment to her carefree life style.

Alfredo's father, who intervenes in their romance for the sake of family honor, manages to make things worse and everyone unhappy. In the end, all are reconciled, but a nearly-impoverished Violetta dies of tuberculosis, which she neglected during her high-style of living.

Theme from Symphony No. 39 (Mozart, K543, 3rd Movement)

DIRECTIONS: There are many changes of hand position. Be sure to follow the fingering carefully.

Learn to play the notes with correct rhythm first. Then, before adding the pedal, play the entire piece using left hand and pedal. The musical form is **A - B - A**. The start of each section is labeled with the letter in a circle.

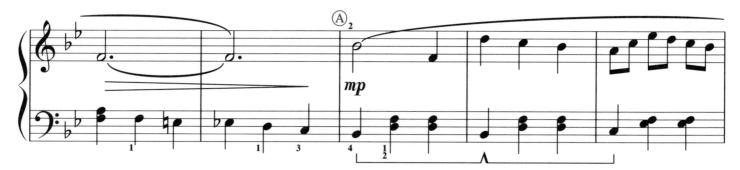

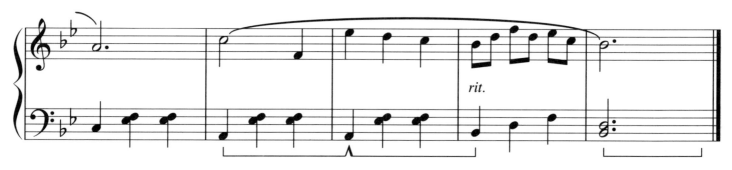

WOLFGANG AMADEUS MOZART (MOE-tsart) 1756-1791 — Austria

Mozart wrote his last three symphonies, Nos. 39, 40 and 41, between June and August of 1788. *During the same three months* he composed a string quartet, two piano-string trios, a piano-violin sonata and a piano sonata !

Parallel Thirds
The left hand plays *parallel thirds* (three successive intervals of a 3rd moving in the same direction) in measure 8. Special fingering enables you to play them legato.

America The Beautiful (Ward)*

DIRECTIONS: Watch for two changes of clef in the bass staff — in measures 8 and 12. The new treble clef leger note "A" is used in measure 9. Check the front reference page for its keyboard location.

There are many changes of hand position. Be sure to watch the fingering carefully.

Learn to play the notes with correct rhythm first. Then, before adding the pedal, play the entire piece using left hand and pedal.

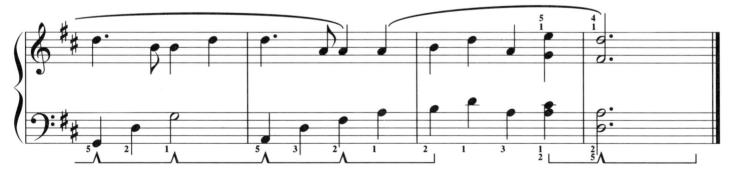

* STORY of "AMERICA THE BEAUTIFUL"

The lyrics for "America the Beautiful" were originally a poem by Katherine Lee Bates, written in 1895. It is based on recollections of a trip to the western United States, which she had made two years earlier. At the time, she was a professor of English literature at Wellesley College in Massachusetts.

Her poem has been set to dozens of melodies. The most successful of these is the one used here, the American hymn tune "Materna," written by Samuel A. Ward in 1888. Ward was a composer and musical instrument dealer in Newark, New Jersey.

You are now ready to progress to **Piano For Adults, Level 3**.

REFERENCE PAGE and MUSIC DICTIONARY — (also see Front Inside Cover)

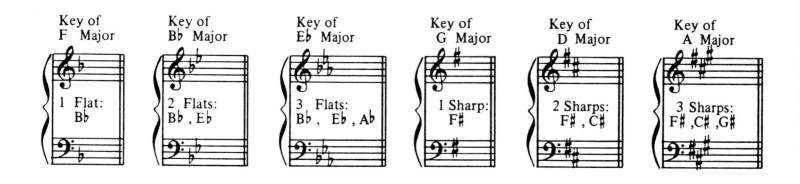

MUSIC DICTIONARY
(Also see Index, page 48)

Most musical terms are Italian, because music writing began in Italy. The accented syllable is shown in *capital* letters.

See the Front Reference Page for illustrations of basic music elements and correlation of notes with their keyboard location.

Terms listed here are limited to those commonly found in Level One methods and supplements. For a more complete listing get the Schaum **DICTIONARY OF MUSICAL TERMS**. With over 1500 words in 96 pages, it contains most terms found in program notes for recordings, concerts and newspaper reviews, including the most used Italian, French, and German words. It is helpful in relations with band and orchestra instruments, vocalists and choral groups.

---

accent (ACK-sent) Stress or emphasis on a note or chord.

accelerando (ahk-sell-er-ON-doh) Becoming gradually faster in *tempo*.

accidental (ack-sih-DEN-tal) Sharp, flat, or natural that does *not* appear in the key signature.

adagio (ah-DAH-jee-o) Slow, slowly.

allegretto (ah-leh-GRET-toh) A little slower than *allegro*.

allegro (ah-LEG-grow) Fast, quickly.

andante (ahn-DAHN-tay) Moderately slow.

animato (ah-nee-MAH-toh) Lively, spirited.

a tempo (ah-TEHM-poh) Return to previous *tempo* (usually following *allergando, ritardando,* etc.)

andantino (ahn-dahn-TEE-noh) A little faster than *andante*.

basso marcato (BAH-so mahr-CAH-toh) Emphasize the bass notes.

beam Thick line connecting the stems of two or more 8th notes.

cantabile (cahn-TAH-bil-lay) Singing style.

chord (KORD) Simultaneous sounding of three or more tones.

common time 4/4 meter. Time signature is: **C**

con brio (kone BREE-oh) With vigor, spirit, or gusto.

cresc. Abbreviation of *crescendo*.

crescendo (cre-SHEN-doh) Gradually increasing in loudness. Also abbreviated with the sign: ◁

D.C. al fine (dah KAH-poh ahl FEE-nay) Return to the beginning and repeat, ending at the word *fine*.

degree Number given to each note of a major or minor scale in ascending sequence.

dim. Abbreviation of *diminuendo*.

diminuendo (di-min-you-END-oh) Becoming gradually less loud. Also abbreviated with the sign: ▷

dissonance (DISS-uh-nunce) Combination of simultaneous musical sounds that are unpleasant or harsh to the listener.

dolce (DOL-chay) Sweetly, softly.

duet (doo-WHET) Music for two performers.

dynamic marks Same as *expression marks*.

enharmonic Writing the same musical *pitch* in two different ways, such as C♯ and D-flat.

espressivo (ehs-preh-SEE-voh) With expression and emotion.

expression marks Signs used to show different levels of loud and soft. For example, *f* and *p*.

extension dot A dot placed to the right of a note head that increases the duration of the note.

fermata (ferr-MAH-tah) Hold or wait on a note or chord, longer than its normal duration. Symbol: 𝄐

f Abbreviation of *forte:* loud.

ff Abbreviation of *fortissimo:* very loud.

fine (FEE-nay) End.

flag Short curved line attached to the right side of a stem. A quarter note is changed to an 8th note by adding a flag.

form The organizing and structure of music, usually labeled in outline form, for example, A-A-B-A.

forte (FOHR-tay) Loud, strong. Abbreviation: *f*

fortissimo (fohr-TISS-ee-moh) Very loud. Abbreviation: *ff*

giocoso (jee-oh-KOE-soh) Humorously, playfully.

half step The interval from one key (of a keyboard) to the next closest key, black or white.

interval Distance in sound between one note and another.

inversion Regrouping of the notes in an *interval* or *chord*.

key signature One or more sharps or flats at the beginning of each staff, next to the clef. See page 46.

largo (LAHR-goh) Very slow, solemn.

legato (lah-GAH-toh) Notes played in a smooth and connected manner.

leger line (LED-jer) Short horizontal line placed above or below as an extension to the musical staff. Used for writing of individual notes beyond the normal range of the staff. Middle C is written on a leger line. See page 29.

leggiero (led-jee-AIR-oh) Light, delicate.

L.H. Abbreviation of *left hand.*

lento (LEN-toh) Slow, but not as slow as *largo.*

maestoso (my-ess-TOH-soh) Majestic, dignified, proudly.

major scale A pattern of whole and half steps in the following order: 2-whole steps, one half step, 3-whole steps, and one half step. See pages 18-19.

melodia marcato (mel-OH-dee-ah mahr-CAH-toh) To emphasize the melody notes, usually in the treble.

metronome (MET-roh-nome) Device to determine tempo or speed in music; measured in beats per minute. See page 4.

mezzo forte (MET-zoh FOHR-tay) Medium loud; softer than *forte.* Abbreviation: *mf*

mezzo piano (MET-zoh pee-YAH-noh) Medium soft; louder than *piano.* Abbreviation: *mp*

mf Abbreviation of *mezzo forte:* medium loud.

minor Chord, melody, or scale often having a sad, mysterious, or spooky sound.

misterioso (miss-teer-ee-OH-soh) Mysteriously.

M.M. Abbreviation of Maelzel's metronome. See *metronome.*

moderato (mah-dur-AH-toh) At a moderate tempo or speed.

mp Abbreviation of *mezzo piano:* medium soft.

musical form See *form.*

note head The round part of a musical note.

octave (AHK-tiv) Interval of an 8th; the top and bottom notes have the same letter name.

octave higher sign The number 8, followed by a broken line and placed *above* a series of notes. Indicates notes to be played one octave higher than written.

octave lower sign The number 8, followed by a broken line and placed *below* a series of notes. Indicates notes to be played one octave lower than written.

op. Abbreviation of *opus.*

opus (OH-puss) Unit of musical work usually numbered in chronological order. May be a composition of any length from a short single piece, a collection of pieces, to a full symphony or opera.

p Abbreviation of *piano:* Soft.

phrase (FRAZE) Group of successive notes dividing a melody or accompaniment pattern into a logical section. This is comparable to the way sentences divide text into sections.

phrase mark Curved line, placed over or under groups of notes, indicating the length of a phrase. The notes of a phrase are usually played *legato.*

pianissimo (pee-ah-NISS-ee-moh) Very soft. Abbreviation: *pp*

piano (pee-YAA-noh) Soft. Abbreviation: *p*

pianoforte (pee-yaa-noh-FOR-tay) Original full name for the *piano,* chosen because it was the first keyboard instrument to effectively play in a wide range of dynamics; thus the combination of words *piano* and *forte* (literally: soft-loud).

pick up One or more notes, at the beginning of a piece which are less than a complete measure. Often called *up-beat notes.*

pp Abbreviation of *pianissimo:* Very soft.

presto (PRESS-toh) Very fast, faster than *allegro.*

repertoire (reh-per-TWAR) Musical compositions previously studied, mastered, and currently maintained by a musician or musical group so that performance can be given with a minimum of preparation.

rest A symbol for silence placed in the staff. A rest shows where and how long NO note is to sound.

R.H. Abbreviation of *right hand.*

rit. Abbreviation of *ritardando.*

ritard. Abbreviation of *ritardando.*

ritardando (ree-tahr-DAHN-doh) Gradually getting slower in tempo.

root 1) Key note of a chord, the same as the letter name of a chord symbol. 2) Lowest note of a root position chord.

root position The position of a triad or chord in which the *root* note is on the bottom and the other notes are stacked above.

scale Sequence of musical tones collectively forming a key or tonality, usually named after the starting tone. See page 18-19.

scale passage Portion of a scale.

semplice (SEMM-plee-chay) Simple, plain.

slur Curved line, placed over or under groups of notes indicating *legato.* Often the same as a *phrase mark.*

staccato (stah-KAH-toh) Short, detached, separated. Indicated by a dot *above or below* a note head.

staff Group of five horizontal lines used for note placement.

stem Vertical line attached to a note head.

step The distance from one musical letter to the very next letter.

tempo (TEMM-poh) Rate of speed used for musical beats or meter.

tempo di marcia (TEMM-poh dih MAHR-chee-ah) March time.

tempo mark Word or words at the beginning of a piece of music explaining the rate of speed to be used. For example, *allegro, andante, moderato.*

tie Curved line that connects two notes on the same line or space that are next to each other. The values of the tied notes are added together joining into one continuous sound.

time signature Two large numbers, above each other in the staff, at the beginning of a piece of music. The *upper* number tells how many counting numbers or beats are in each measure. The *lower* number tells which kind of note gets one counting number. If the lower number is 4, the *quarter note* gets one counting number. See pages 14 and 30.

tonic (TAHN-ik) Starting note or first degree of a scale.

tranquillo (trahn-KWILL-oh) Tranquil, quiet.

transpose (trans-POZE) To play a melody or chord in a different key, starting on a higher or lower note. When transposing, a different key signature and hand position are used.

triad (TRY-add) Chord with three notes.

upbeat (UP-beet) See *pick up.*

vivace (vee-VAH-chay) Lively, quick.

vivo (VEE-voh) Lively, animated.

whole step The distance from one key (on the keyboard) to another with *one key in between* (black or white). The same as two *half steps.*

Suggested SHEET MUSIC SOLOS